This Book Belongs To

_____

_____

this book is dedicated to
Parker Pendergrass

Copyright 2015
DreamWordZ
Productions

written and illustrated by
Mark D. Pendergrass
with Rhandi Pendergrass

Waylon & Stogie
name/logo
and
Animadelphia
are property of DreamWordZ

special guest appearance by
Dexter McDinky Davis
as the marshmallow roaster
owned by
The Davis Family, Tupelo, MS

The Slippery Slope
is a work of fiction. Any resemblance
to real people, places, or
events is purely coincidental.

ISBN-13: 978-0692460542
ISBN-10: 0692460543

DreamWordZ
P R O D U C T I O N S

DreamWordZ
presents

WAYLON & STOGIE

in

The SLIPPERY SLOPE

written and illustrated by
Mark D. Pendergrass
with Rhandi Pendergrass

Everyone in Animadelphia was digging out
from under the biggest winter storm
anyone could remember.

The snow was piled as high as
a Doberman's eye.

Before long, every youngster in
the neighborhood was outside
having fun.

"Hey, everyone!" Stogie called down the street, "It's a snow day! Why don't we go climb Slippery Slope and sled down to Bitterman's Pond?"

"That's a great idea!" they shouted.

As some of the kids went to grab their sleds, Waylon appeared from his house carrying a large snow shovel.

"Come on, Waylon!" cried Stogie. "We're heading to Slippery Slope Park for some sledding."

"I can't right now," said Waylon. "I promised to help Mrs. Thidgewhistle shovel her driveway so she can get to the store."

"Are you kidding?" said Stogie. "Working on a great day like this?"

"I promised," Waylon answered. "But maybe I'll join you after I finish."

"By then, it'll be too late," Stogie said with a frown.

"Let's get going, guys."

"I have an idea," said Cotton.
"Why don't we help Waylon
first and then
go sledding?"

"Perfect!"
said Warren, looking
around to see if anyone else was willing to help.

"Hold on," shouted Stogie. "The snow is already losing its fluffiness. I say we go to the slope before the whole day is ruined."

"The snow will still be there after we finish," said Lucia. "I say we ALL help Waylon and Mrs. Thidgewhistle before we hit the slope."

At that, everybody shouted,
"Let's help Waylon and Mrs. Thidgewhistle!"

...everyone, that is, but Stogie.

Stogie was angry. Nothing was going his way.

"Come on Stogie," said Tiny.
"If you help too, we can get it done much faster."

"I'm not changing my mind," said Stogie. "You can waste *your* snow day but I'm not gonna waste *mine*."

Suddenly, Stogie found himself standing alone. Everyone else was following Waylon down the street to help Mrs. Thidgewhistle. So without even a wave, Stogie turned on his heel and headed toward Slippery Slope Park.

When he arrived, Stogie realized that Slippery Slope was a lot steeper than he had remembered.

For what seemed like hours, he struggled, pushed, and pulled his way up until he stood at the very top.

From there he could see the entire town;
including all of his friends who
were working away at
Mrs. Thidgewhistle's
house...

What losers! he thought.

...and on the other side, he could see all the way down to the frozen surface of Bitterman's Pond.

Yikes! he thought. *That's pretty scary. I wish my friends were here.*

But no one was around except for an ice fisherman at the bottom of the hill.

Just as Stogie got up enough
nerve to try the slope,
his feet began to slip,
and he and his sled
disappeared over
the edge.

Faster and faster he
began to slide, until
he was traveling at
the speed of a
falling boulder.

Meanwhile, Waylon and all of Stogie's other friends were working quickly to clear the snow from Mrs. Thidgewhistle's driveway.

"I sure wish Stogie was here," Waylon said. "He's missing a great time!"

Just then, Mrs. Thidgewhistle stepped out
of her house and threw a snowball at Waylon.

Before you could say *shivering snowflakes*,
everyone was laughing, and snowballs were
flying everywhere.

Back at Slippery Slope Park,
Stogie was still speeding his
way toward the bottom
of the hill.

When he finally reached the edge of Bitterman's
Pond, the snow drifts formed a launching ramp,
sending Stogie and his sled high into the air.

As he came down, Stogie's little round body smashed right onto a thin sheet of ice.

DANGER
THIN
ICE

The ice snapped and cracked as the front of his sled went straight into the freezing water below.

The ice was very slick and Stogie's tiny hands were so frozen that no matter how hard he tried, he could not pull his sled out of the cold water.

Every time he moved, the ice would crack a little more. If someone didn't help him soon, he was going to wind up as frozen as an ice cube.

DANGER THIN ICE

The ice fisherman tried to reach Stogie with a long branch... but it wasn't quite long enough.

"Don't move!" the ice fisherman said to Stogie. "I'll go for help!" At that, he jumped on his scooter and raced into town.

Waylon and his friends were on the road to Slippery Slope Park when the ice fisherman came barreling over the hill.

"Hurry up!" he yelled. "There's a kid stuck on the ice at Bitterman's Pond!"

Upon hearing that, they began to run as fast as they could to Slippery Slope Park.

When they arrived, things were looking very bleak. Waylon and his friends could hardly believe it was Stogie who was in so much danger.

"I'll save you, old buddy!" Waylon shouted.

"Be careful!" said the ice fisherman. "That ice is mighty thin."

Sure enough, when Waylon stepped onto the ice, it began to crack under his feet.

At that moment, Waylon realized it was going to take teamwork to save his very best friend.

"Come on guys!" he said, "That's our friend out there and we need to do whatever it takes to save him."

DANGER THIN ICE

So from the biggest to the smallest, they made
a chain out onto the ice, until they were just
a hand's reach away from the poor,
unfortunate Stogie.

With one final effort—just as the ice was about
to give way—they pulled him out of the
freezing water and onto dry land.

As Stogie sat shivering in front of a warm fire, he was grateful that he had friends who were willing to help him…even when he had not been willing to help them.

For the rest of the day, everyone went sliding down Slippery Slope—at a respectable speed, of course—and there was plenty of fun and hot chocolate for all.

THE END

...time to read it over again!

"If one falls, the other can help his friend get up.
But how tragic it is for one who falls, if
there is no friend to help him get up."

email
waylonandstogie@att.net

visit
www.facebook.com/Waylon.Stogie
www.colorspiracy.com

Waylon & Stogie

www.ingramcontent.com/pod-product-compliance
Lightning Source LLC
Chambersburg PA
CBHW041550040426
42447CB00002B/116